Walking Guen

Gary Williams

SUSPENSE PUBLISHING

WALKING GUEN
By Gary Williams

PAPERBACK EDITION
* * * * *

PUBLISHED BY:
Suspense Publishing

PUBLISHING HISTORY:
Suspense Publishing, Digital Copy, December 2018

ISBN: 978-0-578-43070-6

Cover Design: Shannon Raab
Cover & Interior Photographer: Gary Williams
Paws: Serhii Brovko / iStock

Walking Guen

Gary Williams

It is an honor to represent the citizens of the oldest city in the United States, but when you have articulate and well-informed constituents like Guen, the job is a delight. Her daily patrolling of the town and her careful observations do much to inform the policies of our town—most of all because she truly "doesn't have a dog in the fight." Thank you, Guen.

Nancy Shaver,
Mayor, City of St. Augustine

A Little History

In 2013, my wife and I, our cat, 22, and yellow Labrador retriever, Guen, moved to the beautiful, historic town of St. Augustine, Florida. We fell in love with the city years before, and as a writer, I thought it would be a great place to continue my craft. I soon began walking Guen through the charming, old streets in the early morning hours. Living downtown, there were so many roads to traverse, so many interesting sites to see, that each day became a new adventure.

In time, I began taking photographs of Guen on our walks with my flip phone, often (and purely by accident) capturing the ambiance of the neighborhood and its historic highlights. It was always interesting to see what Guen would find on our walks: things like bubble wrap, articles of clothing (you know how those crazy college kids are), old furniture left out for pick-up, and tennis balls outside the tennis courts. As we continued our daily walks, a bond formed between man and dog. In time, she began "talking" to me and developed a unique personality. No, I'm not crazy, but if you've ever owned a dog, or any pet for that matter, you know exactly what I mean. They have a way of looking at you that makes it easy to read their minds, or at least makes you think so.

Every so often, I would post our photos and small tidbits of our "conversations" on two St. Augustine-centric Facebook pages: I Love St. Augustine & We Love St. Dogustine. Over time, the posts (Guen, really) developed a following. I was surprised when a page administrator emailed me one day and asked if I was going to post a "Guen walk." He had several people wondering why I had missed a day. Understand, I did not commit to a daily post. That was never my intent, nor was it a paying gig. I already had a full-time job writing novels, but each morning as we strolled the city, I realized there was always something whimsical that we would come across, some punny situation, or some frivalous topic that we could share. Thus, the once-a-day 'Walking Guen' posts were born. Now, mind you, these aren't deep, intellectual conversations. Some would say we live in the land of triviality. Guen and I purposely stay away from hot topics such as religion, politics, and the name of Beyonce's children. We keep to lighter subjects such as Guen's love of dog treats, firemen, and attention. We occasionally comment on fashion and food, maybe even a movie or television show, and often tell bad jokes. Although, sometimes we do educate on local history. Mainly, we have fun, and make fun of each other, and surprisingly, people seem to like to follow along with our antics; so much so, that in 2017, a local magazine named me "Person of the Year" in St. Augustine. Of course, I shared the cover with Guen, a/k/a "Dog of the Year."

Never in my wildest dreams did I think Guen would capture the attention of so many with her wit and snarkiness. Not only has she somehow managed to garner thousands of followers—known as Guenablers—but they duly assigned her the title of Queen, in reference to Queen Guenevere of the King Arthur legend.

Special thanks to my writing partner, Vicky Knerly, for her input into this book. I also want to thank Sherry Gauspohl for reviewing, and kudos to Monica Davis and Joe Desiderio for the front and back cover photographs, respectively.

I would also like to give a big thank you to the administrators of I Love St. Augustine & We Love St. Dogustine Facebook pages for allowing me a vehicle by which to reach thousands of folks who have come to adopt Guen and I into their daily lives, and thanks to all of those who bring Guen treats, gifts, and affection. This compilation of the best of our walks from January to June 2017 is a tribute to all of you who have shown us your enduring love and continue to venture the historic streets with us.

So without further ado, let's get the "walks" under way.

~Gary & Guen

January 1, 2017

While walking Guen through the cold, historic streets of St. Augustine this morning, we came upon a couple. We talked, and they introduced themselves. Then Guen introduced herself, but before I had the chance, Guen cut in and said, "This is Christopher."

I smiled at the couple and said, "No, my name is Gary." When they left, I turned to Guen. "I know what you just tried to do."

"What do you mean?"

"If they saw us out again, you wanted them to say, 'Look, there's Guen and Christopher Walken.' "

"I have no idea what you're talking about," she said, breaking eye contact and resuming our walk.

January 5, 2017

While walking through the historic streets of St. Augustine, Guen and I passed the college tennis courts at the corner of Valencia and Riberia. "Guen, did you know that in 1908, Henry Flagler commissioned his last construction effort in St. Augustine on this spot? He built a YMCA. I believe it lasted until the 1970s."

Her eyes widened. "Of course," she exclaimed, "the construction workers on Malaga, Sheriff's Ghost Walk Tours, the police department on King Street, the National Guard Armory, Daytona Bike Week, Osceola's incarceration at the Castillo. Flagler clearly was a man of vision."

"What are you talking about?"

"Construction workers, cowboys, cops, soldiers, bikers, Native Americans. He was preparing for the Village People."

January 7, 2017

While walking through the historic streets of St. Augustine, we were heading south on Sevilla Street, when we heard a bird squawk. As we turned onto Riberia, a man approached us with a large parakeet on his shoulder. I said, "Good morning."

Instead of returning the greeting, he felt obliged to point at his bird and say, "Bird poops on my shoulder."

My response was to point to Guen and say, "I'm glad mine doesn't do that."

January 8, 2017

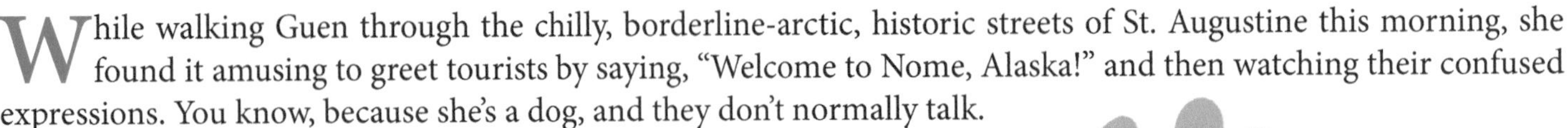

While walking Guen through the chilly, borderline-arctic, historic streets of St. Augustine this morning, she found it amusing to greet tourists by saying, "Welcome to Nome, Alaska!" and then watching their confused expressions. You know, because she's a dog, and they don't normally talk.

January 9, 2017

While walking Guen through the icy, historic streets of St. Augustine this morning, to my chagrin, she found a strip of bubble wrap. I was freezing, but she refused to leave until she had popped each and every last one. Yeah, man's best friend.

January 10, 2017

While walking Guen through the historic streets of St. Augustine this morning, she must have noticed the extra pep in my step. "What are you so excited about?" she asked.

"It's release day for our new novel, *Collecting Shadows*. I always get excited on release day."

"I don't see the big deal. I wrote a book once, you know."

"Yeah, I remember the manuscript: '48 Ways to Make Dog Treats Out of Human Food.' If I recall, 46 of the recipes required prime rib, and the other 2 called for prime rib and lobster."

She responded, "Hey, it wasn't called '48 Ways to Make Dog Treats Out of Human Food on a Budget.' "

January 12, 2017

As we began our foray this morning, venturing through the magical labyrinth of streets in ancient St. Augustine (the wording was Guen's idea to make our walk sound more mythical), we were constantly slowed as Guen sought out those who give her treats.

"Seriously, Guen, you're not going to get treats every day. If I didn't know better, I would say you're starting to have entitlement issues."

She looked at me in astonishment. "You know, I don't need this type of negativity in my life. If this keeps up, I may have to let you go."

January 13, 2017

While walking Guen through the historic streets of St. Augustine this morning, we reached the college. Guen spotted a guy strolling leisurely across the grounds eating an ice cream cone. She did a double-take, then turned to me. "Did you see that? Was that student—"

"Yep, eating ice cream at 7:20 in the morning," I finished her thought.

Guen had a glazed look in her eyes. "This. *This* is why I want to go to college."

January 14, 2017

While walking Guen through the historic streets of St. Augustine this morning, we reached the Visitor Information Center when it began to rain. She turned and glared at me. "Really? You took me for a walk knowing it was going to rain?"

"Hey, don't blame me. The weather report only showed a 15% chance of showers."

"Yeah, and there's only a 15% chance I'm going to complain the entire way home."

"It's going to be a long walk back to the house, isn't it?"

"You have no idea."

January 18, 2017

While walking Guen through the historic streets of St. Augustine this morning, for the third day in a row, she led me to the barbecue restaurant on Cordova Street.

"Guen, I know what you're hinting at in your not-so-subtle way."

"About time."

I shook my head, "Not going to happen. A, they're not open. B, they don't let dogs inside."

She cocked her head and responded, "A, I can wait, and B, Hello?! Takeout."

January 19, 2017

After walking Guen through the historic streets of St. Augustine this morning, we returned home.

"Let me be the first to congratulate you," I said.

"What are you talking about?"

"You successfully located 11 AVs (short for "Attention Victims" a/k/a people who stop to pet her.) It was a record-setting performance. With hard work and dedication, you might just qualify for the next Olympics."

She smirked, "You need to work on your sarcasm. It's not there, yet. And it wasn't 11, it was an even dozen."

January 21, 2017

While walking Guen through the historic streets of St. Augustine this morning, I noticed officials were preparing the neighborhood for a run.

"What's going on?" Guen asked.

"It's a 5K run."

"What's that?"

"It's where people pay an entrance fee to be able to run 3.1 miles."

"Wait. People pay a fee so they can run?"

"Yep."

She shook her head, "It's said that the definition of insanity is doing the same thing over and over, and expecting different results. I think we have a new definition."

"Don't knock it, Guen. It's good exercise."

She didn't respond, and I noticed she was fixated on something up the street. "Wait, are those firemen?" she asked.

"Yes, they're putting up blockades to stop traffic to protect the runners."

She looked at me and grinned.

"Guen, for the love of God, please don't ask them again for their 2017 calendar."

January 22, 2017

While walking Guen through the historic streets of St. Augustine this morning, we reached Orange Street. Guen turned to me and pointed to the Ann O'Malley's sign. "Deli & Pub. I'll make you a deal. I'll take the Deli side, you can have the Pub."

"You just got treats from two different people on our walk, and you're still hungry? Besides, it's a little early for a beer, Guen, which means you're not getting anything from the deli."

She rolled her eyes. "That's a selfish way to start off the week."

January 25, 2017

While walking Guen through the historic streets of St. Augustine this morning, she started to wrap her leash around a tree.

"Um, Guen, don't ignore physics."

She stopped and looked at me with a worried expression. "What'd you say?"

"Physics. It's what prevents the leash from magically passing through the tree trunk."

"Thank God," she wiped her brow, "I thought you said physical fitness, like you were suggesting I go on an exercise regimen or something."

"You know, that's not a bad idea. We could put you on a diet and—"

She cut me off and threw up her paws in confusion. "*Que? No hablo inglés, señor.*"

January 28, 2017

While walking Guen through the icy, frost-bitten, historic streets of St. Augustine this morning, I said, "Guen, we need to have more deep, intellectual conversations. No more talk of squirrels, tourists, or why the sun is on fire. No more puns. No more whimsical, snarky remarks. We need to elevate our thinking, converse on more pressing social issues—profound topics, like global warming, politics, maybe even religion. What do you say?"

She turned to me. "Are you trying to make me stop talking? Is that it?"

January 29, 2017

While walking Guen through the historic streets of St. Augustine this morning, she stopped dead in her tracks on Francis Field. I followed her eyes and spotted a male college student wearing insanely tight blue jeans; they were drawn up so high that they left his ankles exposed. "What in the world is he wearing?" she asked.

"They're called skinny jeans. It's a trend."

She shook her head, "I understand fashion fads come and go, but this one should never have arrived."

"Let's keep walking, Guen."

She insisted on continuing, "For one, they look silly. Two, it's too cold to be wearing that. And three, they look silly."

"I get your point, Guen."

"Do you think he knows that the fourth grade called, and they want their pants back?"

"Let it go, Guen."

January 30, 2017

While walking Guen through the historic streets of St. Augustine this morning, she remarked, "Human sayings befuddle me."

"I know I'm going to regret this, but why?"

"Because you say, 'When one door closes, another one opens.' "

"It's self-explanatory."

"Yeah, but you also say, 'Opportunity knocks.' How can opportunity knock if the door is already open?"

"I suppose dogs have better sayings?"

"Yep. Like, 'Food is good,' 'Rain sucks,' 'If it smells bad, sniff it anyway.' "

"I see. Blunt and to the point."

"Why beat around the bush? Oops, that's one of yours."

February 1, 2017

While walking Guen through the chilly, historic streets (or as she called it, the frozen tundra) of St. Augustine this morning, she asked, "When will this long, harsh, brutal winter end?"

"It's going to 73 degrees this afternoon, Guen."

"I'm not sure I can make it that long."

"Aren't you being a bit overly-dramatic?"

"Says the guy wearing an undershirt, two shirts, a sweatshirt and a jacket."

"Hey, I have thin blood."

"I wouldn't know about that. Mine's frozen."

February 3, 2017

While walking Guen through the historic streets of St. Augustine this morning, she paused before a sign at Memorial Presbyterian Church. "Organ concert?" she asked.

"Before you say it, no, it doesn't mean someone is playing their spleen."

"Maybe they'll play their liver live?"

"I doubt it."

"I heard the opening act was supposed to be an appendix, but it was removed."

"You can stop any time."

"An esophagus encore would surely get a stomach standing ovation." Then her eyes lit up, "I know. It's a concert by *Heart*! Gosh, I hope they play *Barracuda*."

I sighed, "Me too, Guen. Me too."

February 4, 2017

While walking Guen through the historic streets of St. Augustine, Florida, this morning, we journeyed to Grove Avenue.

"What's with all the lion statues around town?" Guen asked. "They're on both sides of the bridge, at the college, here on this wall, everywhere."

"I'm glad you asked."

"Wait, is this going to be one of your boring history lectures?"

"I'll keep it brief. It's a reference to the man who first arrived here in 1513: Juan Ponce de León. León is the Spanish word for lion, and he had a lion on his personal coat of arms."

"I blame his parents, then," she scoffed.

"What are you talking about?"

"They should have named him Juan Ponce de Canine. Think of all those wonderful dog statues we'd see."

"The Spanish word for canine is *canino*."

"Pataytoe, Putahtoe, you get my point, right?"

"Not usually, no."

February 5, 2017

While walking Guen through the historic streets of St. Augustine this morning, she began to complain. "I'm so hungry. I need treats."

"You're just spoiled because you ran into two nice people yesterday morning who gave you treats."

"But I haven't gotten any today. And I'm famished."

"You'll be fine until we get back to the house."

"I'm getting weak."

"Please, enough of the drama."

"I don't know if I can make it."

"I'm seriously starting to think you need an intervention."

"Fine, as long as they serve dog treats."

February 6, 2017

While walking Guen through the historic streets of St. Augustine this morning, we arrived at St. George Street. A woman approached and asked, "Is this the dog on Facebook?"

"I'm taking the Fifth," I joked, and then admitted, "Actually, yes, this is Guen."

She gave Guen some much-appreciated attention, and then we were on our way.

Guen promptly led me to the Gifted Cork. "Darn, it's closed."

"Why, did you want some wine?" I asked.

"Hey, if you can drink this early, why can't I?"

I was momentarily confused, then it dawned on me. "Guen, I meant I was taking the Fifth Amendment, not a fifth of alcohol."

February 7, 2017

While walking Guen through the historic streets of St. Augustine this morning, she turned to me. "I have a money-making idea: dog treat vending machines. Hear me out. You place them in dog parks, vet's offices, and high-traffic areas where dogs walk their humans. It would make a fortune."

"Where do you come up with these half-baked id—" I cut myself off, then said, "You know, it's not your worst idea."

"Says the man who wanted to invent the 'slap' emoji for social media sites. By the way, you don't have any spare venture capital laying around, do you?"

February 9, 2017

While walking Guen through the historic streets of St. Augustine this morning, I said, "Did you hear about the bones on Charlotte Street? Archaeologists think the remains date from around 1570. Can you imagine? These may be the first settlers to St. Augustine. Spanish soldiers and citizens who sailed with Menendez in 1565. How cool is that?"

She didn't respond.

"Guen, isn't that cool?"

"Huh, what?"

"Isn't it fascinating?"

"Sorry," she began, "I didn't hear anything after 'bones on Charlotte Street.' "

February 10, 2017

While walking Guen through the historic streets of St. Augustine yesterday evening, we were approached by a woman pushing a stroller. To me, it appeared the child was too old for the stroller, but who am I to judge? Anyway, as we neared, the woman veered off the sidewalk and into the street, giving us a wide berth even though there was plenty of room to pass. The woman angled so far out into the road, I was worried they were going to get hit by a passing car.

Guen looked at me as if her feelings were hurt and said, "What? Am I Cujo?"

I couldn't help myself. I looked at the woman, pointed to Guen and said, "You don't need to worry. She's still full from the toddler she ate this morning."

I know, I know. It was wrong, but it did bring a smile to Guen's face.

February 11, 2017

While walking Guen through the historic streets of St. Augustine this morning, we arrived at St. Andrews Court off Cordova Street. It was the first time we'd ever ventured down the narrow, dead-end road.

"I wanted to make sure you got to see this road at least once before we leave," I said.

"Leave?"

"Yeah, now that the research on the book is done, and it's out the door, we're moving back to the big city at the end of this month."

"You…you mean, no more Francis Field? No more beautiful streets packed with elegant historic homes? No more meeting new people who have dog snacks?"

I smiled. "Gotcha. I'm just kidding."

"You're not funny. Was that some weak attempt at a February Fools' joke?"

"There is no February Fools."

"Yeah, right. Have you seen how much money humans spend on Valentine's Day stuff?"

"Point taken."

February 12, 2017

While walking Guen through the historic streets of St. Augustine this morning, I said, "That Christmas weight doesn't seem to be coming off you this year. We might need to—"

She cut me off. "Don't say it."

I did anyway: "Exercise."

She cringed. "That's the second most heinous 8-letter word in the English language."

"I shouldn't ask, but what's #1?"

"Treatless."

"That's nine letters. On another note, you have an appearance at Ayla's Acres coming up this Saturday. Funny to think they hosted Loretta Swit before."

"Hotlips?"

"Yep, now you'll be there. It's like they went from *M*A*S*H* to mashed potatoes."

She glared at me, "I know I should be offended, but strangely, I'm only hungry."

February 13, 2017

While walking Guen through the historic streets of St. Augustine this morning, we journeyed into town, and she did something unique. "Guen, that's the first time you've passed through the Old City Gates. This was part of a wall that fortified the city, and it dates back to the early 1700s."

"Why is it called City Gates if there's no gate?"

"It used to have one."

"Then maybe it shouldn't be called City Gates."

I shook my head. "It's named for what it was, not what it is now. We don't call Venus de Milo, Armless de Milo, or the Roman Colosseum, Dilapidated Roman Colosseum, or Stonehenge, Stone-unhenged."

"Now you're just being pedantic," she replied.

"Pedantic? Are you the one who stole my thesaurus?"

"Certainly not. I may have absconded with it when you were enrapt with one of your TV shows, but I didn't pilfer it."

"Case closed," I replied.

February 14, 2017

While walking Guen through the historic streets of St. Augustine this morning, she turned and said, "So you're another year older?"

I nodded, "Yes, but that means I'm also another year wiser."

"I see dementia is setting in."

"Thanks. On another note, can we please not have the same embarrassment as last Valentine's Day?"

"What do you mean? I was just trying to embrace the spirit of the day."

"Guen, you don't do that by telling everyone Happy VD."

February 16, 2017

While walking Guen through the historic streets of St. Augustine this morning, she paused to sniff a stain at the base of a tree. After a moment, she raised her head and said, “Female. Poodle. About six years old. White fur with a pink bow.” She sniffed it again. “Owner is male, bald, mid-forties, blue jeans and a Polo shirt.”

I’ve always been astounded by her sense of smell, but this was amazing. “You can tell all that by sniffing pee?”

“Don’t be ridiculous,” she pointed, “they’re up ahead.”

February 17, 2017

While walking Guen through the historic streets of St. Augustine this morning, we came across two college students who asked to pet her. As she's prone, Guen was initially timid, but warmed up once the affection started. When they began to walk away, Guen tried to follow.

One girl turned and said, "Sorry, girl, we have class."

I said, "C'mon, Guen. You have no class." It was an unintentional dig, but the girls giggled.

Afterward, we walked in silence for a while. Nearing the house, Guen said, "You know those tennis shoes you bought last week?"

"What about them?"

"You might as well pick up a new pair on the way home today."

February 19, 2017

While being led by Guen on an epic, 1-hour-and-22-minute walk through the historic streets of St. Augustine this morning (if I'd been wearing a Fitbit it would have exploded), we arrived at the grounds of the Castillo de San Marcos.

She said, "I have an observation. Why is it that when you take pictures on our walks, they're grainy and fuzzy? Yet, the pictures people took of me at Ayla's Acres yesterday are sharp and clear?"

"Because I take photos with this," I held up my phone.

"You're still using a flip phone?"

"By choice. I don't want to be one of those people who take a picture of their food in a restaurant before eating."

"But those are the best pictures in the world!" she protested.

"I like my phone."

She shook her head. "The 1990s called"...she giggled..."on your 1990s phone"...more giggling..."and they"... raucous laughter..."want their 1990s phone back."

February 20, 2017

While walking Guen through the historic streets of St. Augustine this morning, I noticed two black marks on her side. I felt them, and they were sticky.

"Guen, what did you get into last night?"

She got an excited look in her eyes. "While everyone was sleeping, I heard a raccoon in the driveway. He was trying to break into your car! I dashed out the front door, through the gate, and chased him up under the car, where I brushed against the oil pan and got two drops of oil on my coat. Unfortunately, the raccoon got away. Still, I think my deeds warrant extra treats today."

For a long moment, I looked at her in silence. "You got into the pantry and spilled maple syrup on yourself again, didn't you?"

"How did you know?"

"Because you don't have opposable thumbs to open the front door and gate."

"*That's* the part of the story you didn't believe?"

"Well, if it's any consolation, it's your birthday. You get extra treats today anyway."

February 21, 2017

While walking Guen through the historic streets of St. Augustine this morning, we arrived at Plaza de la Constitucion. By now, Guen had gone to the bathroom three times, and yes, I'd only brought one bag, which had started to tear on the second pick-up. "Post-birthday fallout," I said in disgust, trying to wipe my hand clean on the grass.

"Don't take this personally, but please don't pet me until you've washed up."

"Just because it was your birthday, you didn't have to eat every treat in sight."

"You're the one with opposable thumbs who opens the packages, remember?"

It suddenly occurred to me. "Oh my God. That makes me—"

"That's right," she cut me off, "you're a Guenabler."

February 22, 2017

While walking Guen through the historic streets of St. Augustine this morning, she convinced me to go to the fire station on Malaga Street. “Guen, I know why you brought me here. You want to gawk at the firemen.”

“Don’t be silly. I’m interested in history. Please show me the bell.”

“I’m glad to see you’ve taken an interest in St. Augustine’s past. This bell is over one hundred years old, from 1902. It was borrowed by the National Park Service in 1939 and hung in a tower of the Castillo de San Marcos until 1965. In 1986 the bell was donated to the—” I paused, “Guen, are you listening to me?”

February 23, 2017

While walking Guen through the historic, soggy streets of St. Augustine this morning, she walked on tiptoes.

"What are you doing?"

"The grass is wet, the dirt is wet, the sidewalk is wet, the street is wet…" On and on she complained.

"Geez, Guen, you act like you belong in Oz with others afraid of melting from a little water."

She looked at me, and gave a false smile. "It's amazing," she said.

"What is?"

"That even with your dry sense of humor, everything is still wet."

February 24, 2017

There won't be a "walking Guen" post tomorrow (Saturday) as Guen has an early vet appointment. So we'll leave you with this picture from last night when Guen told Missy a joke.

As you can see, Missy didn't get the punchline, but Guen thought it was hysterical.

February 25, 2017

While walking Guen through the historic streets of St. Augustine this morning, we were several blocks away from the house when a sharp crack of thunder suddenly rattled the air.

Guen released an expletive, then covered her mouth. She looked up at me sheepishly. “Sorry about the language.”

I looked up in the sky. “It’s okay, Guen. You may have said it, but I think I just did it.”

February 26, 2017

While walking Guen through the historic streets of St. Augustine this morning, we reached Francis Field. "Since the vet said that dirty four-letter word to you yesterday, we'll need to start today," I said.

"What word? You mean…?"

She motioned me down as if unable to say it aloud, and whispered in my ear.

I responded, "Um, no, although you do have the right letters. 'Edit' is the four-letter word that our publisher says that makes me cringe. 'Diet' is what the vet said to you. Funny when you consider they both mean the same thing: reduce and refine."

She shook her head, "I don't find it funny at all."

February 27, 2017

While walking Guen through the historic streets of St. Augustine this morning, we again ventured to Francis Field where she sniffed one of the smaller trees.

"What kind of tree is this?" she asked.

"I believe it's some sort of fir tree?"

"You mean like a Christmas tree?"

"I suppose."

"301 days."

"301 days, what?"

"Until Christmas."

"Seriously, Guen? You're terrible at math. You think 2 plus 18 is 218, but you can figure out the number of days until Christmas?"

She nodded. "It's all about priorities."

February 28, 2017

While walking Guen through the historic streets of St. Augustine this morning, we had reached the grounds of the college when she began talking aloud as if writing in a diary. "Day 4. I don't know how much longer I can take it. These streets seem so desolate, so unforgiving. My strength is waning. No one should have to endure…a diet. The only positive is that the vet said I can gain an extra size."

"He said you should 'exercise,' " I corrected her.

She walked slowly in mock exhaustion. "I. Can't. Go. On... Oh, look, another dog!" she went running off with me in tow.

March 1, 2017

While walking Guen through the historic streets of St. Augustine this morning, she said, "I have a great idea for your next novel."

"Shoot."

"Cats invade Earth in giant spaceships. Two dogs upload a computer virus in the mother ship, which leads to the downfall of the aliens."

"It's been done before. *Independence Day*."

"How 'bout this: These two half-brother dogs—the older one is an autistic-savant—go to Las Vegas. The younger brother—"

"You're describing *Rain Man*."

"Okay, I saved the best for last. Two teenage dogs board a luxury liner in England in April 1912, but when the ship hits an iceberg—"

"*Titanic*. Guen, all you keep doing is substituting dogs for people in the stories."

"Which, by the way, would make the stories WAY better."

March 2, 2017

While walking Guen through the historic streets of St. Augustine this morning, she stopped, looked around, then closed her eyes and licked her face. "I…can't…even," she said in an exasperated tone.

"What?"

"I just can't even."

"What?"

"It's what the teenagers say. It's a sarcastic phrase used when surprised, pleased, scared, happy or mad. You know. I…can't…even."

"I know what the expression means, but what are you referring to?"

"I just can't even," she said again.

My frustration bubbled up. "What? You can't even what?!"

"I can't even tell you because it's way too much fun watching you get annoyed."

I shook my head in defeat. "Now, I can't even."

March 3, 2017

While walking Guen through the historic streets of St. Augustine this morning, we reached the college.

"You know what's great about this area?" she asked.

I responded, "That this college building was once Henry Flagler's opulent Hotel Ponce de Leon, one of the most luxurious hotels in the world when it opened in 1888? That it was one of the first buildings in the U.S. constructed from poured-in-place concrete? That Tiffany glass encircles the cafeteria, and many famous artists of the era painted murals on the ceilings? That Thomas Edison, himself, did the electrical wiring, giving the hotel electricity several years before the White House had it?"

After a long moment she said, "I was going to say that the grass is short and well-manicured, but okay, let's go with that."

March 6, 2017

While walking Guen through the historic streets of St. Augustine this morning, she led me near the Visitor Information Center.

"Why did you bring us here?" I asked.

"I wanted to see if the Rebel Alliance had taken care of this."

I shook my head, "Guen, for the last time, this is the Old Spanish Trail Zero Milestone. This is not the Death Star from *Star Wars*."

She replied in a chalky voice, "If wrong, sorry you'll be."

"Oh, I see. Now you're Yoda lab. I've got some green spray paint at home if you want to full-on embrace the role."

She gave me a sidelong look, "Overreact, you will."

March 7, 2017

While walking Guen through the historic streets of St. Augustine this morning, she was recognized yet again. She turned to me. “Don’t get me wrong, I love the attention. But how come so many people who I’ve never met before know my name?”

“I’ve been posting our walks daily, including our conversations.”

“Well, that’s just ridiculous. Who’s going to believe that I talk?”

“It’s all in fun—”

She cut me off, “It’s deceptive.”

“Yeah, I guess you’re right.” I looked at her for a quiet moment, then said, “You do realize the irony in this conversation, right?”

March 8, 2017

While walking Guen through the historic streets of St. Augustine this morning, she led me to Francis Field. There, she sought out scraps of food left on the ground from last weekend's festival. Each time she picked up a morsel, I shook it out of her mouth. She finally got so annoyed with me that she flopped on the ground and wiggled in a circle.

"Guen, what are you doing?"

"If you won't let me have any food, I'm going to rub it all over my fur," she said defiantly.

"I see. And you realize that means when you're trying to nap today, Missy and the cats will be sniffing you. All. Day. Long."

Her eyes widened. "Uh, oh. I didn't think this through."

March 12, 2017

While walking Guen through the historic streets of St. Augustine this morning, she said, "Let me get this straight. Yesterday, at this time, it was 8:30. Now it's 9:30?"

"That's right. Spring forward."

"Just like that? Humans decide to change time? Where does it end? Is that squirrel up ahead now called an aardvark?"

"Of course not."

"Is that motorcycle now a boat?"

"Now you're just being ridiculous."

"Is this pine tree now a unicorn?"

I decided to play along, "Instead of a dog, we can call you a cat."

She cringed, "You sure know how to kill a good conversation."

March 14, 2017

While walking Guen through the dark, historic streets of St. Augustine early this morning, we were on Carrera Street when a man rode by on his bicycle. I acknowledged him with, "Morning," and he waved back.

Guen turned to me. "Why did you say that?"

"It's short for 'Good morning,' an expression of meeting or parting in the morning. I've always felt that if I say 'Good morning,' some people might feel it's a declaration of how their morning has gone. In that case, it might be perceived as presumptuous, especially if they've had a bad morning. So I reduced the phrase to the simple 'Morning,' giving it no preconceptions."

Guen shook her head. "No, I mean why did you say 'Morning' when it's obviously still nighttime?"

I rubbed my chin. "You make a good point."

"I usually do."

March 15, 2017

While walking Guen through the chilly, historic streets of St. Augustine this morning, we reached St. Andrews Court. A slight breeze stirred, and Guen stopped. She lifted her nose high into the air and squinted. "Current temperature is 45 degrees. Although sunny, the temperature won't climb above 53 degrees today."

"And how do you know this?" I asked.

"Instincts."

"Instincts, huh," I said, following the direction of her eyes, "or could it be that you're looking at the Weather Channel on the TV through that second-floor window?"

"Like I said, I instinctively know where to get information."

March 17, 2017

While walking Guen through the frozen tundra of St. Augustine this morning, she turned to me and asked, "What's *March Madness*? I heard it mentioned on TV."

"It's the college basketball tournament to determine the national champions."

"Huh, I thought it was something different."

"Such as?"

"Well, when the temperature swings from 30 degrees to 80 degrees in one day, I thought *March Madness* was some affliction that Mother Nature had come down with."

March 19, 2017

While walking Guen through—

"Wait," she cut me off. "You always say 'While walking Guen, blah, blah, blah.' Why don't we try something new."

"Such as?"

"I don't know. How 'bout Galivanting with Guen?"

"How about Trolling for Treats?" I countered.

"Guen the Streetwalker?"

"I don't think that's the type of attention you want, Guen. How do you feel about Guen's Jiggling Journey?"

"I don't. Wait, I've got it. Since I like sniffing objects and you like the historical nature of things, how 'bout 'Guen Explores and Gary is History.' "

"Let's just agree to disagree, Guen."

March 20, 2017

While walking Guen through the chilly streets of St. Augustine this morning, we were in town when she did it again. She greeted people we passed with, "Welcome to Nome, Alaska!"

"Guen, you've got to stop doing that. You're going to confuse the tourists."

"You really think they don't know where they are?"

"No, I mean because you're talking. After hearing you, they'll spend their vacation time in St. Augustine seeking psychological help."

"I guess you're right," she giggled, "although it would be funny if they went home wearing clothes that said, 'I visited St. Augustine, Florida, and all I got was this lousy straitjacket.' "

March 21, 2017

While walking Guen through the historic streets of St. Augustine this morning, we reached the brick walkway to the church manse. To her horror, the sprinklers were going, the streams soaking the path. Although Guen loves to swim, she hates having water sprayed on her. Fraught with the horrifying reality of not reaching the porch to beg for a treat, she stopped.

I said, "I believe someone's thrown down the gauntlet. You're going to have to go treatless this morning."

She looked at me in utter dismay. "Have you not met me before?"

March 24, 2017

While walking Guen through the historic streets of St. Augustine this morning, a squirrel crossed directly in front of her path. Guen didn't bat an eye.

"How come you no longer try to chase squirrels?" I asked.

"Am I ever going to catch one?"

"No, and you don't chase after cats either."

"Same reason. Scraps of food on the ground. Now that's my game. 100% of the time I can run those suckers down."

I threw up my hands. "Of course you can. They don't move."

"But the Earth is moving. It rotates."

"Yes, I'm aware. Over a thousand miles an hour. And it's traveling through space at more than 18 miles per second."

Her face lit up. "Wow, I had no idea I was so fast! I feel a little woozy."

March 25, 2017

While walking Guen through the historic streets of St. Augustine this morning, I decided to educate her.

"Guen, did you know the streets around here are named after places in Spain? Valencia, Saragossa, Malaga, Carrera, and Sevilla are all Spanish cities."

"What about Lemon Street?"

"Well, there's always exceptions."

"Good, because for a moment there, I thought you were going to tell me lemons are the national fruit of Spain."

"Don't be ridiculous. Pomegranates are."

"Wouldn't fit on a street sign, would it?"

"Probably not."

March 27, 2017

While walking Guen through the historic streets of St. Augustine this morning, we reached the student center for the college.

"Wait," she started, "you're telling me there's a fast-food restaurant on college grounds?"

"Yep, next to the bookstore inside the student center."

"Another reason I need to go to college."

"Why? So you can major in Dog Treats and minor in Attention Grabbing?"

She shook her head. "Don't be silly. I'd minor in Fire Stations, and, yes, there would be field trips."

March 28, 2017

While walking Guen through the historic streets of St. Augustine this morning, we were strolling along the north side of Carrera Street when I said, "Here's an obscure fact; something a lot of people living here don't know."

"I'm giddy with anticipation," she said in a monotone voice.

"Henry Flagler built a baseball stadium in 1890 that covered the area now bordered by the streets of Carrera, Riberia, Saragossa, and Ponce de Leon Boulevard. Professional baseball teams came down from the north and used it for spring training games. The field lasted until 1910, when the land was sold off and homes were erected."

"By the way, why don't you watch baseball anymore?" she asked.

"Last time I watched a game on TV, you got so frustrated."

"Can you blame me? Each time the announcer said 'the pitcher walked the batter,' I wanted to see how long the leash was, but they never showed it."

March 29, 2017

While walking Guen through the historic streets of St. Augustine this morning, we were strolling along Saragossa Street when she sidestepped a banana peel. "Whew, I barely avoided disaster there."

"Yeah, I can see the headlines now: 'Dog Slips on Banana Peel! Breaks Ego!' "

"You wouldn't laugh when you were saddled with paying my medical bills and the copious amount of dog treats it would take to nurse me back to good health."

"So you think this is a big problem in society today? Slipping on banana peels?"

"I watch cartoons. The struggle is real."

March 30, 2017

While walking Guen through the historic streets of St. Augustine this morning, she noticed one of her favorite houses on Carrera Street was still for sale.

"I should bid 10 dog treats for it. I bet they'd jump at the offer."

"Are you serious?"

"Okay, 12."

"Guen, they're not selling you a 4,000-square-foot, 1903 home that's on the National Historic Register for 12 dog treats."

"Okay, 14. But not one treat more."

"Guen, they don't want dog treats. They want money."

"Shut the front door! What kind of a crazy, upside down society are we living in where money is more valuable than dog treats?"

"Let me put this in an economic context that you can understand. It takes money to buy dog treats."

She grinned. "Like I said, I loooooove money."

April 2, 2017

While walking Guen through the historic streets of St. Augustine this morning, we had to circumnavigate Francis Field because of the Rhythm & Ribs festival.

As we passed by a sign on the fence, Guen said, "Look! I made a shadow puppet!"

"Um, it's not so much of a shadow puppet as it is your real shadow."

"Don't be silly. I'm not that big."

"No comment."

She looked at me with surprise. "That's it. I'm going on a new diet starting today. Only two meals a day, we'll take two long walks a day, and I'll only get half of a dog treat any time I go outside and use the bathroom."

"Guen, that's exactly what you do now. You're not changing a thing."

She was momentarily quiet. "I think it was the angle of the sun that made my shadow look big."

April 3, 2017

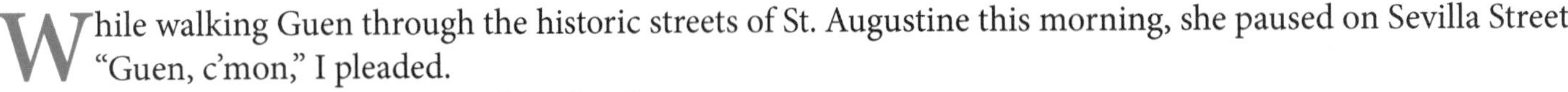

While walking Guen through the historic streets of St. Augustine this morning, she paused on Sevilla Street.

"Guen, c'mon," I pleaded.

"No, I want to see who gets off this bus."

"For the last time, this is not the Mystery Machine, and Scooby-Doo is not stepping off that bus."

She gave me a sidelong glance. "Look at this thing. You think there's any chance a cartoon character is NOT on board?"

"Good point."

April 4, 2017

While walking Guen through the historic streets of St. Augustine this morning…Just kidding. It's raining. She won't budge. Therefore, I'm going to use creative writing and improvise. Here it goes:

While walking Guen through the historic streets of St. Augustine this morning, we had a delightful time discussing Guen's diet, local history, her new exercise routine, her love of the Cats & Firemen calendar—"

"Oh, just stop," she cut me off while looking over my shoulder. "You're making me nauseous."

April 5, 2017

While walking Guen through the historic streets of St. Augustine this morning, she remarked, "Wow, look at all the rain puddles."

"Mother Nature is trying to catch up."

"Speaking of Mother Nature, if she got together with Father Time, would they have a naturally good time?"

I chuckled, "Maybe. And if they had kids, they'd be little sundials."

She looked at me with confusion. "I don't get it."

"You know, sundials. Mother Nature provides the sun, Father Time has the clock. They'll make little sundials."

"That's weak."

"Oh, right. I know you. You'll go home and tell that joke to Missy like it's yours."

She feigned surprise. "I don't know what you're talking about."

April 6, 2017

While walking Guen through the historic streets of St. Augustine this morning, we were on the grounds of the college when she said, "College graduation is coming up at the end of this month, and I'd like to do something to help the seniors get through their finals."

"Really? Aren't you the same dog who, four years ago when the students were incoming freshman, wanted me to convince them your breed was a Bolivian Lollygagger?"

"They're seniors. They've grown, matured."

"Well, then, I'm proud of you for wanting to help out. What'd you have in mind?"

"I want you to tell them of a new tradition: it's good luck to pet me during finals week."

"Why would I tell them that?"

"Because if I talk to them, they'll freak out."

"No, I mean why would I tell them that? Isn't that a bit self-serving?"

"I like to think of it as giving back."

April 7, 2017

While walking Guen through the historic streets of St. Augustine this morning, we moved north on Riberia when we came to the intersection at Saragossa Street. The normal STOP sign was gone, replaced by a much lower one.

"Look, Guen. Just your height. It's like your own personal STOP sign. I think they're trying to block you from getting to Francis Field."

"Yeah, like that's going to happen."

"Hey, maybe the city came up with street signs tailored just for you. We'll know for sure if we see one that says, 'Reduce Speed to 1 mph.' "

"It's a shame, really," she said, shaking her head.

"What is?"

"I remember when you used to be funny."

April 8, 2017

While walking Guen through the historic streets of St. Augustine this morning, we strolled east on Orange Street.

"What is this building?" Guen asked.

"Old Orange Street School. It was built in 1910. It went from being a high school to St. Augustine Junior High, then a grade school, then Orange Street Grammar School, and, finally, Orange Street Elementary School."

"So…what was the purpose of this medieval-looking, small, barren brick room with the iron locked gate?"

"That was a holding cell to lock children in when they misbehaved in class."

She looked at me in shock. "Are you serious?"

I cracked a smile. "No, I believe it was used for storage." Then my expression hardened. "Or maybe it was a dark dungeon to hold pet dogs when kids brought them to school," I said with a sinister laugh.

She backed away, glaring at me. "You're still not funny."

April 9, 2017

While walking Guen through the historic streets of St. Augustine this morning, we were on Almeria Street when she turned to me and asked, “Isn’t today the Blessing of the Treat down at Matanzas Bay?”

“Um, no. Today’s the Blessing of the Fleet.”

“Well, that doesn’t make any sense.”

“And Blessing of the Treat does?”

“Bless a treat, and it might multiply. In my world, that makes a ton of sense.”

“Now you’re being silly,” I said.

“Fleet, treat. Same thing.”

“Yeah,” I nodded, “because every fisherman wants to head offshore on a motorized Milk Bone.”

She gazed off absently. “Wouldn’t that be a thing of beauty?”

April 11, 2017

While walking Guen through the historic streets of St. Augustine, we were on Cordova Street when she said, “I feel bad for Tuesday.”

“Why?”

“Because it has no identity. Other days have cool labels.”

“Oh, you mean like how Monday is ‘Moan-day,’ Wednesday is ‘Hump Day,’ and Friday is ‘TGIF’?”

“No, like ‘Walk-to-Francis-Field-Wednesday,’ ‘Throw-a-tennis-ball-Thursday,’ and ‘Firemen Friday.’ ”

“Let me guess. You propose ‘Treat Tuesday.’ ”

“Well, now that you mention it…”

“I’ve got a better idea. How about, ‘Take-your-dog-to-the-vet-Tuesday’?”

She winced. “On the other hand, this whole notion of labeling days seems ridiculous.”

April 12, 2017

While walking Guen through the historic streets of St. Augustine this morning, she paused to sniff a barbecue grill at the curbside.

"It's a shame, really."

"What is?" I asked.

"The death of this grill. Think of all the history—all the cheeseburgers, hot dogs, and steaks. All the salmon, oysters, and shrimp. The lamb, chicken, and lobster. Maybe we should say a few words."

"Seriously, Guen, it's just a grill."

She looked up at me, wiping a tear from her eye.

"Oh, great. Now you're making me weepy," I said.

For a quiet minute, the two of us stood there, paying our respects. As we walked away, Guen said, "I suddenly have this craving for ribs."

April 13, 2017

While walking Guen through the historic streets of St. Augustine this morning, she turned to me. "I've got a great idea."

"Which absolutely terrifies me."

"I'm being serious. We should open up a bed & breakfast that gives patrons a discount if they bring their dogs."

"It's not your worst idea."

"We could call it Guen's Friends…or, The Guen Inn."

"Wait, is this about benevolence or you wanting to see your name on a sign?"

"I'm not answering that."

April 16, 2017

While walking Guen through the historic streets of St. Augustine this morning, we were passing the college tennis courts on Riberia Street when she said, "Guess what I saw in the kitchen during the night?"

"What?"

"The Easter Bunnies."

"Guen, I hate to break it to you, but the Easter Bunnies aren't....wait, Easter Bunnies? Plural?"

"Yes," she said excitedly, "there were three of them. One was gray, the other two were orange. They watched me from the countertop, oddly, as they licked their fur."

"Guen, those were our cats."

"Couldn't be. I watched them go into the corners to hide colorful eggs while making a strange gagging noise."

"They weren't hiding eggs, they were coughing up hair balls."

She shook her head, "Nah, that's impossible. But as much as I love to eat eggs, in the spirit of Easter, I'll let you try one first."

April 19, 2017

While walking Guen through the historic streets of St. Augustine this morning, we were on Markland Place when she remarked, "The college students we've passed seem more intense, more focused."

"That's because next week is finals week."

"Oh, no. It's coming."

"What is?"

"The return of the Stombies. Student zombies. You've seen them: the slow walk, the ghastly vacant eyes, the mumbling..."

"Well, look on the bright side, Guen. At least they won't eat your brain."

"Yeah, but they may challenge me with practice test questions."

"Oh, the horror."

April 20, 2017

While walking Guen through the historic streets of St. Augustine this morning, I said, "Oops, I forgot to bring a poop bag."

"You mean we have to go all the way back to the house? What if I promise not to go?"

"You can't do that."

"Yes, I can. And you can put that down on paper."

"That's what you said when we potty trained you as a puppy."

"What?"

"You can put that down on paper."

She shook her head back and forth. "New rule. Every time you tell a bad joke, you give me a dog bone. As it stands, you owe me one. But if you want to give me 47, we can bank it for the rest of the week."

"Guen, the week ends tomorrow."

"Good point. We should probably round it up to a cool 50."

April 21, 2017

While walking Guen through the historic streets of St. Augustine this morning, we were on Riberia Street when I said, "You know, 135 years ago we'd be standing in the mud flats of San Sebastian River."

"You might. I wasn't born."

"You know what I mean. Did you ever wonder why most of the streets around here are named after Spanish cities—Valencia, Carrera, Saragossa—but this street is called Riberia?"

"No."

"It's because when Henry Flagler bought this property, known as the Model Land Company Tract, the San Sebastian River reached all the way up to here. He filled it in with dirt to enlarge the land area. Originally called Ribera Street—Ribera is an old Spanish word which loosely translates to 'water's edge'—the name eventually evolved to Riberia Street."

She gave me a sidelong look. "Where we live was once in the river?"

"Yep."

"So, we live on a houseboat?"

"Never mind, Guen."

April 23, 2017

While walking Guen through the historic streets of St. Augustine this morning, we were near the Visitor Information Center when Guen said, “The city should hire me. I could be a guide.”

“Perhaps.”

“In addition to a salary, I’d only require naps at 10, 12, 2, and 4. Oh, and dog treats on the hour.”

“You’re a shrewd negotiator, Guen.”

“We labs are known for our wheeling and dealing.”

“I thought you were known for wheeling in place before going to the bathroom?”

“Tomato, tomahto.”

April 24, 2017

While walking Guen through the historic streets of St. Augustine this morning, I said, “Let’s keep the walk short. I’m feeling under the weather.”

Confusion clouded her face. “Aren’t we all?”

“What?”

“Under the weather. If we were over the weather, there wouldn’t be enough oxygen to breathe.”

I shook my head. “It’s hard to argue with that kind of logic.”

April 25, 2017

There won't be a "Walking with Guen" this morning as I battle the crud. In the meantime, I give you a scene from the other afternoon when Guen stopped, looked to the sky, and allowed the sunlight to spotlight her face as if pondering existentialism. It was such a poetic pose that I felt moved, as if she was silently seeking the answers to our very existence.

"In search of enlightenment?" I asked.

"Nah. Stiff neck."

April 26, 2017

While walking Guen through the historic streets of St. Augustine this morning, Guen had an extra pep in her step as we strolled next to a fence.

"What are you so happy about?" I asked.

"April 18th. It's GDWGWIASW Day."

"What's that?" I asked, taking a sip of my coffee.

"You don't remember?" Just then, Guen walked me between two trees. I immediately hit the spider web, turned into a seventh-degree blackbelt, and flung coffee in a 9-foot radius—with a great deal of it landing on me. Guen laughed so hard, she almost stumbled into the fence.

Wiping my face and arms, I said, "Oh, yeah. Now I remember. Guen-Ducks-While-Gary-Walks-Into-A-Spider-Web Day. I really hate GDWGWIASW Day."

"Yeah, but we should never break from tradition," she giggled.

April 29, 2017

While walking Guen through the historic streets of St. Augustine this morning, once again, she proved she's incorrigible. Guen found a couple of firemen venting a fire hydrant. She thought it was her birthday, Thanksgiving, and Christmas, all rolled into one.

"Guen, seriously. Open your eyes and wipe that smile off your face. Guen? Guen?"

April 30, 2017

While walking Guen through the historic streets of St. Augustine this morning, we passed a girl jogging while talking on her phone. I don't mean a hands-free device, she was running with her phone pressed to her ear.

Guen stopped, turned, then said, "Well that was a first."

"Yeah, for me, too."

"Although I have heard of a new fitness craze—Sprint & Speak. You talk while you run. In this way, you keep your vocal cord muscles in perfect harmony with the muscles in your legs so that you're never off-balance between the upper half of your body and your lower half."

I stared at her. For a moment, she held her deadpan look. Then, slowly, her mouth curled up at the edges and she began cackling uncontrollably.

"You made that up, didn't you?"

"What tipped you off? Was it the absurdity of the concept or my raucous laughter?"

"I'm not talking to you anymore."

May 1, 2017

While walking Guen through the historic streets of St. Augustine this morning, I remarked, “In this neighborhood, we have an Orange Street and a Lemon Street. A few more streets like that, and we could have the fruit salad of roads.”

She looked at me in confusion. “I don’t know where you buy your fruit salad, but mine don’t include lemons. On another note, where are all the college kids?”

“Graduation was Saturday. The underclassmen won’t return until late summer.”

“You mean?”

“That’s right. A mere 110 days before we encounter the first college freshman and we convince them that your breed is a Bolivian Lollygagger. It’s a rite of passage, really.”

She smiled, “And the most magical time of the year.”

May 2, 2017

While walking Guen through the historic streets of St. Augustine this morning, we found ourselves on the bricks of Sevilla Street before Flagler's Memorial Presbyterian Church.

"How old is this building?" Guen asked.

"Built in 1890, the church is 127 years."

"I bet it was really something when completed."

"No doubt."

"Tell me about it."

"Well, I read that it's grandeur took the citizens of St. Augustine by surprise, from its Basilica style to—"

"No," she cut me off, "I mean give me your firsthand point-of-view."

I sharpened my eyes. "Guen, for the last time, I was not alive then."

May 3, 2017

While walking Guen through the historic streets of St. Augustine this morning at zero-dark-thirty, I said, "Guen, please turn toward me so I can take your picture."

She frowned. "No. When are you going to get a smartphone?"

"My goal is to be the last man on Earth with a flip phone."

"That's very self-centered."

"How is that self-centered? It's MY phone."

"Because you're taking MY picture. And everyone knows the flip phone camera adds 10 lbs."

"That's a television camera, Guen."

"Same thing," she huffed.

May 4, 2017

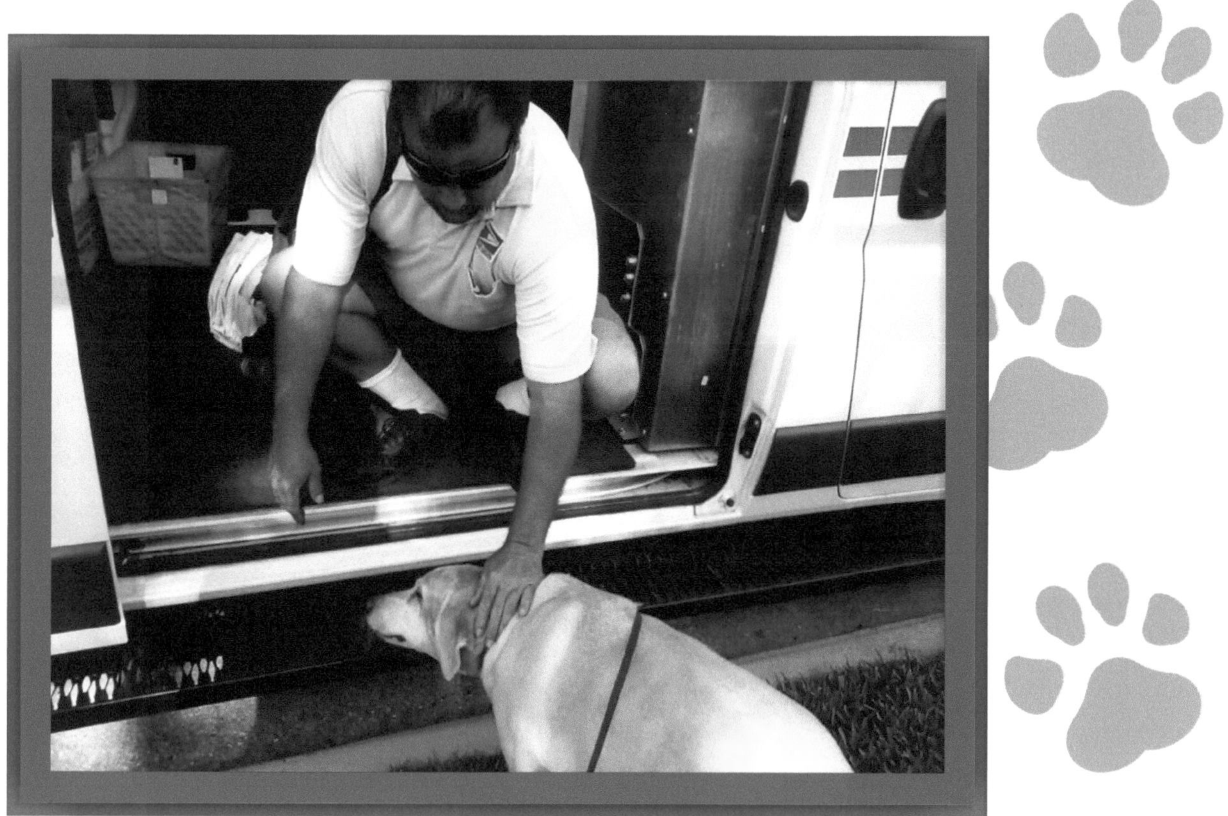

While walking Guen through the historic streets of St. Augustine yesterday afternoon, Guen found our friendly mailman. It's said: "Neither snow, nor rain, nor heat, nor gloom of night stays these couriers from the swift completion of their appointed rounds." Unfortunately, the Mailman's Motto forgot to factor in the disruptive abilities of Guen.

I apologize to everyone in the neighborhood who may have gotten their mail late.

May 9, 2017

While walking Guen through the historic streets of St. Augustine this morning, she said, "I'm still freaked out by these bright yellow curbs. Doesn't St. Augustine have a history of Yellow Fever outbreaks?"

"Yeah, but the last occurrence was in the 1880s. Before that, the worst case was in 1821. Quite a few people buried in Huguenot Cemetery next to the Visitor Information Center were victims of that outbreak."

Her eyes grew large. "The curbs turning yellow could be a precursor to a Yellow Fever epidemic."

"Nope, it's just yellow paint."

"Well, it's pretty obvious these bright yellow lines are following me with malicious intent."

"I see therapy in your future, Guen."

May 10, 2017

While walking Guen through the historic streets of St. Augustine this morning, we were on Cordova Street passing the barbecue restaurant when I commented, "Seeing that makes me hungry."

"Ever notice the location of this restaurant?" she asked.

"What do you mean?"

"It's directly across the street from Tolomato Cemetery."

"What about it?"

"I'd love to be a server on the outside deck. When someone ordered ribs, I'd say 'My apologies, we're out at the moment.' Then make a furtive glance toward the cemetery, and say, 'Or maybe not…' "

I stared at her for a moment. "I'm suddenly not hungry any more."

May 15, 2017

While walking Guen through the historic streets of St. Augustine this morning, Guen turned and asked, "Why did that lady scowl at you?"

"Oh, she thinks you went #2 and I didn't pick it up."

"But I peed."

"A lot of people don't realize a female dog squats to do both."

"Ironic, considering a female human—"

"Stop," I said.

"Here's a suggestion. Next time this happens, look them dead in the eyes, and say, 'I haven't yet mastered the ancient and delicate Chinese art of extracting urine from the earth with a plastic bag.' "

I gave her a look of admonishment. "Guen, that's dripping with sarcasm…and I think I'll use it."

May 16, 2017

While walking Guen through the historic streets of St. Augustine this morning, she asked, "How's the new manuscript going?"

"Good. We deliver it to the publisher in August."

"Have you considered the idea I gave you for the next book?"

"You mean the one about the superhero dachshund named Edgar from Tupelo, Mississippi, who's clad in a royal blue cape and wearing a 1942 gray fedora with a tail that's actually a magic wand that he uses to help other animals in distress and whose parents were Albanian refugees?"

She shook her head in disgust. "You never listen to me. I said black cape, not royal blue."

May 17, 2017

While walking Guen through the historic streets of St. Augustine this morning, she blurted out, "Bacon."

"Huh?"

"Bacon."

"What?"

"Bacon."

"Guen, why do you keep saying bacon?"

"I can't help it. I have bacon on my mind."

"Okay, let's talk about something else. Did you see how fast that squirrel ran? He shot off like a missile."

"Did you say 'sizzle?' "

"Sometimes you can be very trying."

"Did you say 'frying?' "

"Please keep walking. You're makin' me crazy."

She wheeled around excitedly, "Did you say, 'You're bacon me crazy?' "

May 19, 2017

While walking Guen through the historic streets of St. Augustine this morning, we were on Riberia Street when I remarked, "I'm surprised this house is still for sale. It was built by Henry Flagler in the late 1800s."

"Obviously, it's haunted," Guen said.

"Don't be ridiculous. There's no such thing as ghosts."

"Well, you may not believe, but I do. And while we're on this topic, it bothers me when people talk about loved ones who've departed and say, 'I'm sure they're looking down on me right now and smiling.' "

"You wouldn't find that comforting?"

"Are you kidding? It means that when you die, you have to watch the equivalent of reality TV. I can't stand it for one hour a week, and now I have to watch it for eternity?"

I nodded. "You do make a good point."

May 20, 2017

While walking Guen through the historic streets of St. Augustine this morning, we were returning home when I said, "TGIF, Guen."

"What does that mean?"

"It stands for Thank God It's Friday. Or, in your case, after getting treats from two nice people on our walk, it means The Guen Is Full."

She yawned. "More accurately, it stands for The Gary Isn't Funny."

May 21, 2017

While walking Guen through the historic streets of St. Augustine this morning, I had to pause to clean off my shoe from something I stepped in. Yeah, you guessed it.

Anyway, I said, "Guen, before this street was Saragossa, it was named Sebastian Avenue. See that home?" I pointed across the way to a two-story, yellow house. "That's known as the Ritchie House. It was once owned by Henry Ritchie. He's credited with drawing the first detailed, birdseye view of St. Augustine in the late 1800s."

"Bird's-eye view? If you want to impress me, how about drawing a dog's-eye view?"

"Yeah, that's what I want to see. The streets as they appear from 14 inches off the ground."

She smirked. "At least then you might see what you're about to step in."

May 22, 2017

While walking Guen through the historic streets of St. Augustine this morning, she said, "I had the best dream ever. I was a food critic invited to eat for free in a brand-new restaurant that was inside a fire station, and all the waiters were firemen. They were bringing me courses of bacon, lobster, bacon, ice cream, bacon, steak and more bacon. Then Missy nudged me, and I woke up."

"I was about to do the same. You were smacking your lips in your sleep."

She eyed me incredulously. "It was unlimited bacon. What don't you understand? Even dream-bacon is more awesome than most real foods."

May 25, 2017

While walking Guen through the historic streets of St. Augustine this morning, she said, "Look. Someone's hiding underneath this tarp."

"Yes, Guen, someone in the shape of a motorcycle."

"Don't be ridiculous. No one would hide in the shape of a motorcycle. It's obviously a Minotaur."

"The mythological half-bull, half-man creature? Geez, you're right. I don't know why I didn't see it."

She shook her head confidently. "I know, right?"

May 26, 2017

While walking Guen through the historic streets of St. Augustine this morning, she said, "Tell me what you think about this: 'Able to eat a dog treat in a single bite. Able to gawk at firemen from a great distance. Able to nap most of the day away. It's the return of…The Treat Seeking Missile!' "

"You want to know what I think? I think your superhero tagline needs a lot of work."

She shook her head. "Everyone's a critic."

May 27, 2017

While walking Guen through the historic streets of St. Augustine this morning, she paused to drink water from a clean puddle on a lot.

"Speaking of water," I began, "do you know why Bridge Street behind the Lightner Museum, a/k/a Hotel Alcazar, is called Bridge Street?"

"No. Wait, I mean, yes. You don't need to tell me anymore."

"Too late. Lake Maria Sanchez once reached all the way to King Street. Back then it was called Maria Sanchez Creek. At the time, Bridge Street contained a bridge which arched over the creek. As Flagler prepared to build the Hotel Ponce de Leon (now Flagler College) and Hotel Alcazar, he capped the creek way back, turning it into a lake. Still, the area where he planned to build the Hotel Alcazar was more swamp than land, and he was forced to stab some 4,000 tree logs into the earth to help stabilize it."

"So, Bridge Street really had a bridge, thus the name?" she asked.

"That's right."

"It's a shame the bridge is gone."

"Why?"

"I'm ready to jump off it."

May 30, 2017

While walking Guen through the historic streets of St. Augustine this morning, she turned to me and said, "I propose a process improvement initiative."

"A process improvement initiative? What are you? Corporate America?"

"Hear me out. Instead of giving Missy and I a treat when we return from our walks, you could give them to us before the walks. That way, you won't have to worry about forgetting."

I looked at her suspiciously. "You're banking on me forgetting I gave you a treat before we left, so then I give you another one when we return—in essence, giving you guys a Milk Bone BOGO. Might as well call your plan the Mooch Pooch Initiative."

She turned away, "Hey, just tryin' to help out."

May 31, 2017

Whilst walking Guen through the fabled streets of St. Augustine this morning, we reached the college student center, when Guen unexpectedly took a seat. "I do beseech thou. I doth need a mild reprieve from our journey, lest I waste away."

"Tired?" I asked.

"Tis so."

"That's because you expended all your energy begging for a treat from the ladies at the church."

She cocked her head. "Twas a worthy endeavor, was it not, my knave?"

"That's a matter of opinion. By the way, why are you talking like a Shakespearean play?"

"I hath no idea what injustice thou art accusing me of."

"Not accusing. Methinks if I turn on Netflix, I'll find that thou recently watched *Romeo & Juliet* or *Othello*." I paused. "Oh, crap, now you've got me talkin' like Macbeth."

June 1, 2017

While walking Guen through the historic streets of St. Augustine this morning, we reached the Ancient City Baptist Church parking grounds when she took a seat.

"What now?" I asked.

"It's a sit-down protest. This is the start of hurricane season, right?"

"Yep, June 1st."

"And humans set this calendar window of June through November."

"Well, it's based on weather patterns and the highest probability of having weather conditions conducive to generating a hurricane."

"But since humans set the start date of June 1st, it can be pushed back until September 1st. That way, we'd only have a three-month window instead of six."

I started to argue, then reconsidered. "I'll tell ya what. I'll pass your suggestion on to the National Hurricane Center."

"Thank you," she said, standing up.

As we continued our walk, I said, "I can't help but notice you didn't attempt a hunger strike."

"Don't be ridiculous."

June 3, 2017

While walking Guen through the historic streets of St. Augustine this morning, she said, “Do you know what today is?”

“No idea.”

“It’s National Repeat Day. It’s National Repeat Day.”

“Ha, ha. Very funny.”

“It’s a great day we should all celebrate. It’s a great day we should all celebrate.”

“You can stop now.”

“Stop what? Stop what?”

“You’re going to do this all day, aren’t you?”

She gave a villainous smile. “Until midnight tonight. Until midnight tonight.”

June 5, 2017

While walking Guen through the historic streets of St. Augustine this morning, she said, "After I went to the bathroom and you picked it up, I heard you tell that man walking by that I'd left you a 'gift.' Jeez, if I had known that's what you'd accept as a present, I could have saved a lot of money at Christmas and your birthday."

I stared at her in stunned silence. "Um, Guen, let's not exchange presents this year."

June 6, 2017

While walking Guen through the historic streets of St. Augustine this morning, she cautiously approached a bike and addressed it, "Do you come in peace?"

"What are you doing?"

"This thing must be extraterrestrial. Nothing on Earth is this green. I'm trying to understand its intentions for coming to our planet."

"Guen, it's a moped."

"In that case, you may have to go back in time to stop the moped uprising."

"Okay, you need to stick with either the *Terminator* or *The Day the Earth Stood Still* theme, but please don't mix the two. It gets too confusing."

She stared at me. "Seriously? You're an author. You should be able to keep up."

June 7, 2017

While walking Guen through the historic streets of St. Augustine this morning, we were on Sevilla Street when I said, "On Cordova Street, next to the Tolomato Cemetery, there's an oak tree with a palm tree growing out of the center of it. It's dubbed the 'Love Tree.' There are at least seven trees in St. Augustine where two separate species of tree grow in, on, and through one another." I pointed into a side yard and continued, "See that tree? It also has a palm growing out of an oak. While the Cordova Love Tree is in a heavy tourist-traveled area, this one is obscure."

Guen nodded. "I see. So, if you don't want the public love, you come to the west end of Saragossa and get private, discreet love."

"Or unrequited love, since it loves without getting any attention in return."

"And if you climb to the top of this tree, lose your grip, and tumble to the lower branches, you can say you fell in love."

"Why is this conversation starting to sound like a seedy romance novel?" I asked.

"Hey, you brought it up."

About the Author

Gary Williams lives in St. Augustine, Florida, with his wife, Jackie. When he's not walking Guen, his yellow Labrador retriever, he's writing full time. His passions include history, sports, and fishing.

To date, he and his co-author, Vicky Knerly, have published eight novels and one short story with *Suspense Publishing*:

Death in the Beginning (The God Tools: Book 1)
Three Keys to Murder
Before the Proof – A Samuel Tolen short story
Indisputable Proof (A Samuel Tolen Novel: Book 1)
Manipulation
Evil in the Beginning (The God Tools: Book 2)
End in the Beginning (The God Tools: Book 3)
Collecting Shadows
Blood Legacy (A Samuel Tolen Novel: Book 2)

If you're interested in becoming a "Guenabler" too, check out all her merchandise at https://www.cafepress.com/guenablermerchandise.

CPSIA information can be obtained
at www.ICGtesting.com
Printed in the USA
BVHW022317020119
536938BV00014B/207/P